Gazetteer

CORNWALL
†Gwennap Pit SW 7241
†Breage SW 6128
†St Hilary SW 5531
[EH] †Tintagel SX 0789

DEVON
†Exeter SX 919925

DORSET
†Ackling Dyke SY 02Z178
†Badbury Rings ST 964030
†Dorchester SY 94900
[NT] *Hod Hill ST 856106
†Jordan Hill SY 698821
[EH] *Maiden Castle SY 669885
Material from here and other Roman
sites in or near Dorchester displayed in
the Dorset County Museum, Dorchester
†Maumbury Rings SY 693902
  Poundbury. A late Roman Christian
  cemetery SY 683912
  Spetisbury Rings ST 915020
†Woodcuts ST 9618

GLOUCESTERSHIRE
†Blackpool Bridge SO 653087
[NT] *Chedworth SP 053135
[EH] *Cirencester SU 016955 Corinium
  Museum, Amphitheatre SP 020014
*Gloucester SO 8318 Gloucester City
  Museum has an outstanding Roman
  collection
[EH] †Great Witcombe SO 899142
*Lydney SO 6152Z6
†Sea Mills ST 551758
†Wadfield SP 0226
[NT] *Woodchester SO 840030

HAMPSHIRE
†Bitterne SU 420120
  Bokerley Dyke SU 015200
  Bramdean SU 6228

†Winchester...

...terial
Museum

ISLE OF WIGHT
*Brading SZ 599863
†Combley SZ 538878
†Newport SZ 500880

SOMERSET
*Bath ST 317564 Bath Roman Museum
  Charterhouse ST 506561. Material from
  here is displayed in Wells Museum
  Fosse Way. A large part of this is now
  replaced by modern highways but a
  good stretch survives as the A37 for most
  of the route between Shepton Mallet
  and Ilchester
  Ilchester ST 520226. Material from here
  is displayed in Ilchester Museum and
  Somerset County Museum, Taunton
  Castle
†South Cadbury Castle ST 628252.
  Material from here is displayed in
  Somerset County Museum, Taunton
  Castle and Yeovil, Museum of South
  Somerset
†Wookey Hole ST 531480. Material from
  here is displayed in Wells Museum

WEST SUSSEX
*Bignor SU 988147
†Chichester SU860050 Chichester
  District Museum
*Fishbourne Palace SU 841047

WILTSHIRE
  Devizes Museum SU 620780
[EH] †Old Sarum SU 137327
*Salisbury and South Wilts Museum
  SU 300300

---

*An important or specially interesting site which it is well worth making an effort to visit
†A site where there is still something of interest to be seen, but which is not in the
premier category

Before the Romans came

'Britannia, that land completely separated from the world'

VIRGIL

OPPIDUM A generic term in Latin loosely meaning town. The Romans used it to denote the native settlements defined by earthworks and natural features which were a characteristic of Late Iron Age Britain.

The British islands have always been magnets for immigrants, many of whom have arrived first in the area which today we know as Wessex.

At the time of the first Roman invasion, in 55 BC, eastern Wessex was dominated by a number of Celtic tribes collectively known as the Belgae, who had begun to cross the Channel, from what is now northern France, a mere 50 years earlier. The details of their territorial arrangements are not entirely clear, but we can identify the Atrebates of Hampshire, and a particularly aggressive tribe, or group of tribes, known as the Catuvellauni, in the middle Thames Valley, Buckinghamshire and Hertfordshire with a capital at St Alban's. The Late Iron Age culture of the Belgae gave them a relatively high standard of living. They were skilful farmers, who used slave labour to shape the landscape into patterns that lasted for many centuries. (One of their farmsteads has been imaginatively recreated at Butser Hill, near Petersfield in Hampshire.) Their nobles were men of wealth who enjoyed the use of luxuries from the Mediterranean. Their kings ruled from large townships which, though they lacked the trappings of Roman civic life, were substantial centres of trade and industry.

The Belgic tribes pressed hard against their neighbours in western Wessex, in particular the Durotriges of Dorset and the Dobunni of Gloucestershire,

who were descended from earlier, Bronze Age, immigrants. These tribes appear to have been more loosely organised than the Belgae, as confederations of petty chiefdoms, each of which was focussed on a fortified hilltop, such as those to be seen at Hambledon Hill and Maiden Castle in Dorset. Their culture, while it showed the influence of their more advanced neighbours, was not so rich; their farming was less organised and productive, their craftwork less sophisticated. But they were hardy warriors, and difficult people to repress.

Iron Age tribes in Wessex when the Romans arrived.

The Roman Invasions

'They fought thirty battles, crushed two warlike tribes and captured more than twenty fortresses'

SUETONIUS

The early stages of the Roman occupation of Britain were tentative and uncertain. Julius Caesar launched what he subsequently suggested was a reconnaissance in force in the year 55 BC, but his force of 12,000 heavy infantry did little more than land in Kent before returning within a few weeks to Gaul. Caesar may have felt that his military reputation needed strengthening after this foray; in the following year, he assembled an army of 30,000 legionaries, 2,000 cavalry and unknown numbers of auxiliaries, in more than 800 ships, for a determined attack on the Belgic tribes of south-eastern England. He stormed through Kent, defeated the dominant Catuvellauni under their king Cassivellaunus, and imposed an obligation to pay annual tribute to Rome, before returning with honour, as he felt, satisfied.

Britain was not seriously troubled again by Rome until AD 43, when the emperor Claudius, newly elevated to an insecure throne, sought military prestige through the conquest of a new province for the empire. His general, Aulus Plautius, landed in Kent with 24,000 legionaries and perhaps the same number of auxiliaries, and fought at least two severe battles before being joined by Claudius himself for a final push to the capital of the Catuvellauni, which was then at Colchester – after which Claudius returned to Rome and glory.

Over the next four years, between AD 43 and 47, the legions fanned out in a remorseless pattern of conquest. The Second Augusta, under the future emperor Vespasian, may have landed at Chichester and were sent westwards into Wessex, where they 'fought thirty battles, crushed two warlike tribes, and captured more than twenty fortresses' (Suetonius). Relics of this savage warfare have been found at numerous sites, including the hill forts at Spettisbury Rings, Maiden Castle, Hod Hill and Worlebury.

By the end of the year 47 the Romans had tightened their grip on everything south and east of a line drawn from the mouth of the Severn to the mouth of the Humber – a line marked by their great military road, the Fosse Way. The wealth to be extracted from this fertile lowland zone would probably have satisfied their ambitions; but they were under constant threat from the north and west, where lay lands of a different sort. 'Roman nerves frayed here: wars were long, booty meagre, glory hard-won, and the accounts did not balance' (Neil Faulkner). In the end, the barbarians beyond the pale were to succeed in pulling down the gilded image of Roman Britannia.

The Emperor Vespasian.

**CLASSIS BRITANNICA
The Roman naval fleet which patrolled the English Channel.**

Left above: *Iron Age sling stones.*

Left below: *Hod Hill Iron Age camp with a Roman fort built into the north-west corner.*

The Roman Army

'Rome was a society organized for war'

Once the lowland zone had been conquered, there would have been little call for the continuing presence of these battle groups. However, Britannia continued to demand the presence of more troops than almost any other Roman province, because of the never-ending difficulty of controlling the northern parts of the island. During the governorship of Agricola (78–85) a traditional war of manoeuvre was attempted against the wild tribesmen, but increasingly thereafter the doctrine of the massed offensive gave way to one of dispersed defence – as the Hadrian and Antonine frontier fortifications,

the subsequent walling of towns in southern England, and the still later forts of the Saxon Shore, all demonstrate. These strongholds were garrisoned by ever-smaller units of men armed and trained to fight behind cover, often with the aid of projectile-firing machinery. Such mobility as could be mustered was provided by heavily armed cavalry units – and these were the new elite. But the cavalrymen of the later Roman army were not themselves Romans, as the legionaries had been (in theory at least); they were more likely to have been recruited from the invading hordes whom they were paid to oppose.

Towns were about the same size as medieval Salisbury. They sometimes grew up as civil settlements outside the new forts.

Basic military rations seem to have consisted largely of grain for porridge and bread, bacon, cheese, salt, olive oil, vegetables and sour wine. Beef, mutton, venison and chicken were also eaten, and fish and shellfish if available.

AUXILIARES Soldiers in a Roman army unit originally recruited from among conquered peoples, often with specialised skills.

Throughout most of the history of the Roman empire, more than half of the entire revenue of the state was spent on the army. Rome was a society organised for war, depending on war as the means by which wealth was acquired and distributed. So long as there were rich territories to be conquered and plundered, Rome prospered; when military marauding ceased to return a profit, decline set in.

The story is clearly illustrated by the differences between the army which Claudius sent to Britain in AD 43 and that which was withdrawn by Constantine III in 407. The invaders came as a field force of heavy infantrymen who fought in close, massive formation, stabbing with short swords from behind a shield-wall which was itself a battering-weapon. This army moved through hostile territory at up to 30 miles

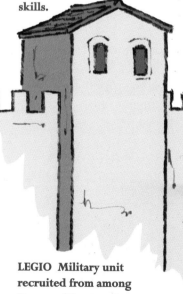

LEGIO Military unit recruited from among Roman citizens and generally used for strategic purposes during the imperial period. The legion was divided into ten cohorts, each nominally 500 strong.

a day, like a great, self-sufficient predatory beast – the legions built their own fortified camps, constructed military roads and bridges, and supplied all their own needs of commissariat, logistics and munitions. In support were auxiliary troops, sometimes in profusion – archers, slingers, spearmen and cavalrymen – but these were provincial mercenaries, whereas the legionary had to be a Roman citizen.

LIMITANEI Garrison troops holding regional fortresses.

COMITATENSES The mobile field army of the later empire.

A Client Kingdom

'They sent their armies to subdue, control and exploit the riches of the province'

The Romans, unlike some of the Europeans who acquired empires in the nineteenth century, were not much concerned with emigrating from their homes to settle in new lands. They sent their armies to subdue, and thereafter to control, the native tribes, but their objective was to exploit the riches of the conquered provinces, not to populate them with Italians. Where possible, therefore, imperial policy sought to make agreements with native rulers who would undertake to support the Roman power, send regular payments of tribute, and generally manage their affairs in the interests of Rome.

Collaboration could be rewarded in many ways, the most potent of which was access to the Roman lifestyle. Archaeological evidence makes it clear that the Belgic tribes of southern England were keen to acquire Mediterranean luxuries well before the invasion of AD 43, and the emperor Claudius – or, more probably, his man on the spot, Aulus Plautius – appears to have been quick to strike a bargain with at least one native ruler.

This British 'Quisling' was Cogidubnus, or Togidubnus, king of a branch of the Atrebates known as the Regni. He was granted Roman citizenship, and must have been generously subsidised; in return he evidently 'delivered' a large area of central southern England and is known to have remained loyal during the revolt of Boudicca in AD 60–61.

The owner of Fishbourne Palace, Cogidubnus, in return for supporting Vespasian following the death of Nero in AD 68, was accorded the title legatus augusti, *which enabled him to sit in the Roman senate. An inscription recording this title, unique to a client king, can be seen in the wall of the Assembly Rooms, Chichester.*

The value attached by Rome to Cogidubnus' support can be seen in the magnificent remains of his great palace at Fishbourne, near Chichester, a building which must have been designed by a Roman architect; it covers an area roughly equivalent to that of the main block of today's Buckingham Palace in London. The opulence of this royal establishment is staggering – and while much of the material was, of course, imported, it also conveys a telling idea of the wealth to be found in Britannia at that period.

LEGATUS The emperor's personal representative in a province who commanded the army, had judicial power and watched over local government.

Urbanising the Aristocracy

'The toga was everywhere to be seen'

TACITUS

COLONIA A town founded by Rome to house those who held Roman citizenship, perhaps retired legionaries.

MUNICIPIUM A native town rewarded by Rome with special rights of citizenship.

Roman civilisation flourished in city air, and imperial policy set a high priority on encouraging town life in the newly conquered province of Britannia. The historian Tacitus summed up the matter, with characteristic sour cynicism, in his life of Agricola: 'Agricola had to deal with men who, because they lived in the country and were culturally backward, were inveterate warmongers. He wanted to accustom them to peace and leisure by providing delightful distractions . . . He gave personal encouragement and public assistance to the building of temples, piazzas and town-houses . . . he gave the sons of the aristocracy a liberal education . . . they became eager to speak Latin effectively . . . and the toga was everywhere to be seen . . . And so they were gradually led into the demoralising vices of porticoes, baths and grand dinner parties. The naïve Britons described these things as "civilisation", when in fact they were simply part of their enslavement.'

Winchester in Roman times.

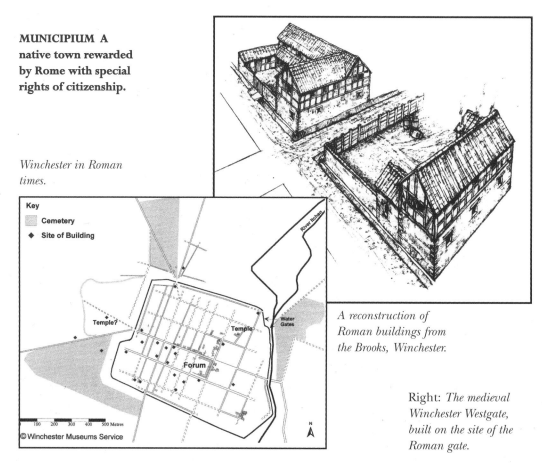

Key

Cemetery

◆ Site of Building

Temple?

Temple

Water Gates

Forum

River Itchen

100 200 300 400 500 Metres

© Winchester Museums Service

N

A reconstruction of Roman buildings from the Brooks, Winchester.

Right: *The medieval Winchester Westgate, built on the site of the Roman gate.*

Archaeologists have uncovered impressive remains of this process of urbanisation in the area of Wessex at Chichester, Winchester, Dorchester, Exeter, and especially at the tribal capitals, Cirencester and the 'lost city' of Silchester. At the height of their prosperity, in the second and early third centuries AD, these were true towns, with populations of several thousand people. Their streets were laid out on grid-plans, they boasted temples, theatres, baths and market-places, and, most important of all, they were the residences of the ruling class and the centres of government.

Aristocratic wealth: gold finger rings from Silchester.

A reconstruction painting of Roman Silchester by Alan Sorrell.

Part of the remaining city wall of Silchester.

As in other provinces of the empire, however, the towns of Britannia proved to be hothouse plants, unable to endure harder conditions. There is evidence of over-extension in programmes of municipal construction work before the end of the second century, and when the burden of centrally imposed taxation intensified in the third century, the governing class whose presence was essential to the effectiveness of civic life appear to have slid away from the towns, and returned to the country-dwelling habits of their ancestors.

The imperial authorities may have tried to check the trend during the later third century through the building of fortifications to make the towns attractively secure. Many of these town walls were massive in scale and strength, but they were symptoms of decline, not prosperity. Their eventual ineffectiveness is starkly demonstrated at Silchester, where the walls survive but the town has disappeared.

Villas

'No retreat from the Roman lifestyle'

COLONI Peasant labourers of the late empire who were required by the law to remain on their landlord's property.

A reconstruction drawing of Rockbourne Roman villa by Mike Codd.

The migration of the Romano-British aristocracy in the third century from the towns to the countryside had less to do with a preference for rural life than with a need to escape from intolerable burdens. The imperial government, which had begun by offering magistracies as incentives to the Celtic warlords to live in towns, had made office-bearing an obligation – and hereditary, so unavoidable. Worse still, the town magistrates, or decurions, had been declared liable to make good out of their private means any shortfall in the tax revenues demanded by Rome.

If, however, as seems likely, the country-dwelling aristocrat was able to save on his tax bill, he was evidently happy to spend all the more freely on Roman-style luxuries for his own enjoyment. The remains of the villas which stud the south-facing slopes of Hampshire and Berkshire, Dorset and Gloucestershire, provide evidence of great wealth and real sophistication; there was no retreat from the Roman lifestyle. Nor – surprisingly – is there evidence of any gradual decline; on the contrary, it is unmistakably clear that villa owners were commissioning new mosaic floors, bath-houses and hypocaust

systems right through the fourth century, and that on a scale which was, if anything, growing in luxuriousness.

The elegant spaciousness of life attained in the great houses at Chedworth and Woodchester, North Leigh and Rockbourne was not to be rivalled in England until the sixteenth century, at least. Indeed, in some respects the civilisation of the last years of Roman Britain had a positively eighteenth-century flavour.

In a sense, though, the compact, serf-worked farming estates, of which these villas were the physical and administrative centres, looked back to the pre-Roman chiefdoms of the Durotriges – and forward, too, to the warrior-led principalities of the Dark Ages which were to follow.

DECURIO
A magistrate.

Chedworth villa hypocaust.

Roads and Communications

'Much of Britain's modern road system was first laid down by the Romans'

MANSIO A way-station provided for official travellers on the principal roads through the empire.

There are several layers of meaning to be drawn from the saying 'All roads lead to Rome'; one of the simplest is the fact that much of Britain's modern road system was first laid down by the Romans, to aid the advance of their armies and to ensure a steady flow of traffic and communications to and from the heart of the empire.

Archaeological research, supplemented by documentary evidence such as the third-century route book entitled the Antonine Itinerary, and the scroll known as the Peutinger Table, which is derived from a fourth-century original, has established the course of more than 6,000 miles of major Roman roads in Britain, and many more again of minor routes and local tracks. The construction of this network involved much accurate surveying, the records of which survive in the shape of numerous milestones, and skilful engineering, including the construction of many bridges.

The Roman roads transformed economic and social life in Britain, as well as supporting the army's task of controlling the province. Merchants with their goods, as well as troops, couriers and officials moved ceaselessly between the ports and settlements, like the red corpuscles of the Roman bloodstream. Along the main roads, posting stations every twenty miles or so supplied the needs of the imperial mail service; civilian requirements were met by inns and trading places which developed at crossroads and similar key points.

The two principal roads of the Wessex region were the Fosse Way, which ran along the frontier of the province as it was first formed, from Exeter north-east towards Lincoln; and another (which, curiously, has no generally used name for the whole of its length) probably marking the central line of Vespasian's advance westwards from London to Silchester, and thence to the coast at Dorchester.

Roman roads in Wessex.

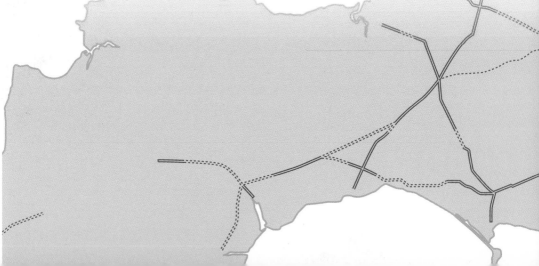

Ackling Dyke. The Roman road between Old Sarum and Badbury Rings, looking east near Oakley Down.

A Roman milestone near Stinsford, Dorset.

Death and Taxes

'A system for extracting wealth for the benefit of the powers in Rome'

CIVITAS The basic unit of Roman government as applied to Roman Britain. Indigenous tribes were designated *civitates* and were treated as though they were city states. Their territory was governed by a central town council drawn from the local landowners.

The Romans were a supremely legally-minded people, with an apparently innate talent for giving remorseless administrative expression to principles of law. They clamped their iron frame so firmly on to the empire that it often survived even after their soldiers had been withdrawn; this was not the case in Britain, but even there, for four centuries, the inhabitants of southern England knew the inexorable quality of Roman order, Roman justice and the Roman tax system.

In the centre of every town, large and small alike, beside the forum or market-place, was a basilica or administrative centre. This was a great hall, the roof of which was often supported within by rows of columns, which created a nave and aisles. At the end of the hall were tribunals, where magistrates administered justice. Punishments in minor matters usually involved fines or confiscations; more serious crimes would be referred to a higher authority, and might lead to sentences of exile or death. Imprisonment was not a usual form of punishment.

Other parts of the basilica were devoted to local administration, carried out under the supervision of imperial officials called Curatores Civitatis – Guardians of the Community. Much of the activity was concerned with the collection and recording of taxes: the empire was essentially a system for extracting wealth from subject provinces for the benefit of the powers in Rome.

It was always the case that actual collection was contracted out, but in the third and fourth centuries tax-gathering became increasingly localised – to the advantage of some, and the disadvantage of their neighbours. During the same period the pay of the army, which was set centrally, rose rapidly – by 125% in one 20-year period, for example. It appears, therefore, that the wealthy villa-dwellers of the Cotswolds in the fourth century, while they may have been in a position to squeeze their own peasantry, perhaps for as much as half of the value of their annual produce in taxes and rents together, were also paying increasingly high premiums for a military insurance which, as events were to prove with startling suddenness, had been issued on a false prospectus.

FORUM The focal public square at the centre of a Roman town which acted as the main meeting-place. In Britain it was usually surrounded on three sides by shops and on the fourth by a *basilica*.

A Mixture of Religions

'The druids take no part in war and do not pay tribute along with the others'

CAESAR

LARES Titulary deities, protectors of a locality.

A votive offering. A Rhenish ware motto beaker reading 'VITVLA' (a pun on the words for bull calf and loved one): third-century pit, Neatham.

A model of the Roman temple at Maiden Castle, Dorset County Museum, Dorchester.

The writings of Caesar, Tacitus and Pliny suggest that the religious practices of pre-Roman Britain were dominated by the Druids; certain early-modern antiquarians, such as John Aubrey and William Stukeley, proposed the Druids as responsible for the prehistoric structures to be found on Salisbury Plain; and the actions of today's eccentrics who gather in white robes at Stonehenge on midsummer morning have deluded numerous people into believing that they are looking at survivals of an authentic ritual. In reality, we know very little about the Druids – other than the fact that they had nothing to do with Stonehenge. They were a priestly caste who exercised considerable power over the Celtic tribes of Britain and Gaul; they worshipped forest gods, and engaged in rites of human sacrifice – sometimes burning victims alive in wicker frameworks. They may have been at the heart of tribal resistance to the Romans, and thus responsible for the massacres at St. Alban's, Colchester and London in 60 AD. Certainly the Roman authorities decided to root them out with a ferocity quite uncharacteristic of their usual tolerant attitude towards native cults. The last Druids were exterminated by Agricola's army in Anglesey in 78 AD.

Celtic religion was mostly concerned with the worship of nature, often in the form of woodland or water deities; the river Severn still bears the name of the goddess Sabrina. Cunomaglus, who had a temple at Nettleton in Wiltshire, was a sun-

Brean Down Roman temple.

A reconstruction of the pediment of the Roman temple in Bath. At the centre is a Gorgon's head (below), powerful symbol of the goddess Sulis Minerva.

god. Nodens, who was celebrated in splendour at Lydney in Gloucestershire, was a hunting god. A shrine in Winchester was dedicated to Epona, a goddess of horses and the underworld. Sulis was a healing deity, powerful at Bath. And the strange, enigmatic trio of little hooded figures known to the Romans as the Genii Cucullati had many shrines in the Cotswolds and elsewhere.

Numerous Celtic deities fitted easily into the classical pantheon, and so were treated as local equivalents to established figures such as Mars, Venus or Minerva. But this did not mean that no differences were recognised ; temples erected by the Romans to their own gods were in Mediterranean, rather than Celtic form, and those dedicated in honour of the deified emperors were especially important as being symbols of the official regime.

As the centuries passed, new forms of religion were imported from distant parts of the empire. The cults of Isis and Serapis came from Egypt, that of Mithras from Persia – and that of Christ from Palestine. Evidence of the presence of Christian believers from the 3rd century onwards has been found at many places in Britain, including, in the Wessex region, Silchester, Cirencester, Chedworth, Frampton and Poundbury. The most important of the early Christian sites is at Hinton St. Mary in Dorset, where Christ is portrayed in a splendid mosaic. Christianity was declared the official religion of the Roman empire in 312 by Constantine, who had actually succeeded to the purple in York – but we should not see anything specifically British in this historic commitment!

CUCULUS A hooded cloak, of a style popular in Britain.

The Frampton mosaic pavement which displays the Christian chi-rho symbol.

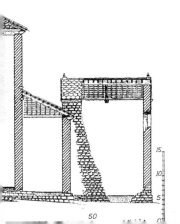

The Trappings of Civilisation

'Bathing and the use of mosaics were widely adopted in Britannia'

Painted head of a girl from Sparsholt Roman Villa bathhouse.

THERMAE Warm springs or baths, natural or artificial.

Laying a mosaic floor.

Many aspects of life in Britannia, at any time during the occupation, would have been found very un-Roman in Rome itself, but at least two of the hallmarks of Mediterranean civilisation were evidently popular and widespread in the province.

Scrupulous attention to hygiene was one of the first requirements of Roman military discipline, and every barracks had its bath-house. Similarly, every town founded by the military authorities featured a communal bath-house at its centre. The municipal baths were places for exercising, socialising and doing business, as well as for washing, and at fortunate spas such as Aquae Sulis (Bath) they had medical functions as well. The freedom to use these baths would have been a mark of a certain position in society, much like membership of a select modern health club.

When the towns decayed, from the third century onwards, the rich who moved base to the countryside took their bathing habit with them. The more luxurious villas boasted several complete suites of baths, suggesting both considerable wealth on the part of their owners, and the possibility of interestingly complex patterns of occupancy.

The use of mosaic work, whether in the lining of baths or as the decorative flooring of dining rooms and other principal apartments, was the other distinctively Roman feature to be widely adopted in Britannia. The inhabitants of the southern part of the province seem to have been particularly addicted to this amenity, which combined the advantages of efficiency and durability with those of display and social assertion, in the highest degree. The remains of urban mosaics have suffered more from the attrition of the centuries than those of the villas, but perhaps in any case the art of the mosaic workers reached its peak in Britain during the period of villa culture, in the third and fourth centuries. The glories of Littlecote, Brading,

The Great Bath at Bath.

Chedworth and Woodchester can still astonish us by their richness and sophistication; they demonstrate the extent to which the workshops of Corinium (Cirencester), which seem to have provided many of the finest mosaics, were organised on a positively industrial scale.

Cupid on a dolphin. One of the mosaics found at Fishbourne Palace, Sussex.

A Roman mosaic roundel depicting the head of Christ, from Hinton St Mary, Dorset.

HYPOCAUSTUM
A bath room, heated from below; more generally, an underfloor heating system.

A mosaic pavement from Sparsholt, Hampshire.

The Economy

'The resources of the island of Britannia were ruthlessly exploited during the occupation'

The population of Britannia lived, essentially, by subsistence farming. But the motive driving Rome's imperial ambition was always, quite explicitly, the search for wealth, and the resources of the island were ruthlessly exploited during the occupation. The tin of Cornwall and the gold of Wales, which had figured largely in the greedy minds of the first invaders, proved accessible only in moderate quantities ; but the lead of the Mendips was mined and exported on a vast scale – it has been identified as a component of the water-pipes of Pompeii, among other places in the Roman world. Still more important to the imperial predators, however, was the silver content of the lead; southern Britain became a major supplier of bullion to the Roman mints. Iron was mined, and worked, chiefly for domestic consumption, in many parts of the country; the Forest of Dean and the Weald of Kent were probably the principal sources of the iron used in the lowland region of the province. In the later years of the occupation, when currency supplies were running short, iron bars seem to have acquired value as capital assets – at least, such appears to be the implication of the two massive pigs discovered in the Roman villa at Chedworth.

Apart from its minerals, Britain exported quantities of agricultural produce, in

particular supplies of corn for the army in north-western Europe; most of this exported corn was grown on vast 'factory farms' in the newly-drained fenlands of what is now Lincolnshire and Cambridgeshire. Other regions, including Wessex, probably exported modest surpluses of agriculturally-based products such as leather and cloth; we know that one particular form of hooded cloak, popular among shepherds in the Cotswolds and soldiers on Hadrian's Wall, was regarded as characteristically British.

The finest pottery used in the western Roman empire was Samian ware from Gaul, but southern Britain developed its own pottery industry at an early stage of the occupation, with centres at Oxford (producing imitation red Samian ware), in the New Forest (poorer, colour-coated Samian-style ware) and Poole (black-burnished cooking pots). The pottery at Poole was the biggest in Britain, though also one of the most primitive in its techniques; its produce was distributed by sea to most parts of the province.

Rebels and Invaders

'Saxon mercenaries under Romano-British aristocrats in Hampshire?'

DUX BRITANNIARUM Commander of the frontier garrisons of northern Britain in the later Roman period – an infantry general.

The Roman occupation of Britain was never a tranquil affair. The Claudian conquest was very nearly overturned by Boudicca's revolt in AD 61, and over the following century the menacing turbulence of the northern tribes compelled the Roman authorities to wage a series of arduous campaigns, and to extend a fortified border further and further into the highland zone. Somewhere around the end of the second century the attempt to keep this northern boundary impenetrable seems to have been abandoned in favour of a policy of defence in depth, which involved the walling of towns both small and large throughout the entire province. This may have been the product of a change in military organisation, from mobile field armies of infantry legions to a mixture of garrison troops with roving cavalry units, rather than a response to immediate invasion threats; but it was not long, in any case, before the new system was tested.

Sea-borne Saxon raiders from the far side of the North Sea began to appear around the coasts of Britain from the early years of the third century, and attacks from Scotland and Ireland also resumed. It may seem strange that it was at this very time that the fortified towns, which must have offered a degree of protection against the marauders, fell into decline, while the

wealthier elements in the population, in southern Britain at least, moved into undefended villas in the countryside. The answer to the puzzle is probably in part that the raids occurred sporadically, rather than continuously, and in part that residence in the towns was made intolerable for the rich by the burden of imperial taxes.

Some historians claim to have detected evidence of Saxon mercenaries being retained by Romano-British aristocrats in Hampshire and the Thames Valley in the fourth century. Whether or not this was the case, more substantial protection was provided for the inhabitants of the region by the system of watch-towers, forts and naval bases strung round the south-eastern and southern shores of England during the later third century. The great citadel of Portchester is perhaps the most impressive, and best preserved, of these 'Forts of the Saxon Shore'.

In the end, it was not so much the pressure from without, as the removal of the garrison troops to participate in civil wars on the European mainland, that caused the collapse of Britannia. And the province itself played no small part in fomenting these fatal wars. In 193 the governor Clodius Albinus led his legions in an attempt on the imperial throne; he invaded Gaul and was killed in 197. The years 286-96 saw a so-called 'British empire', first under Carausius and then Allectus, until the latter was defeated and killed by Roman forces under Constantius – whose son Constantine, in his turn, made a successful bid for the throne. Another would-be usurper, Magnentius, appeared briefly in Britain in 306. Finally, Magnus Maximus made Britain the springboard for his almost successful attempt to seize the empire in 383-8 ; his stripping of the garrisons was not quite the last stage in the dismantling of the Roman military machine in Britain, but it established the pattern that was to be followed, with terminal consequences, in 407-10.

Portchester Castle, the best preserved of the Saxon Shore Forts, was part of a strong line of defence against invaders.

The Legacy of Rome

ROCKBOURNE ROMAN VILLA · BATH · WOODCHESTER · BRADING

'The villages retreated from the marching-lines of the war-bands'

Opposite:
End of Empire. A reconstruction painting, by Mike Codd, of scavengers at the abandoned Roman villa of Rockbourne.

The Roman presence in Britain always resembled an exotic plant struggling to survive in an alien climate. When it died, it left traces of its existence, but little in the way of fruits.

The fortified towns, with their mansions and baths, were partly resettled by people with primitive lifestyles, who often built their huts on the streets for the sake of the foundations, while they used the ruined Roman buildings as cattlesheds and pigsties. The villas, with their mosaics and hypocausts, were deserted or degraded; cooking-fires blackened the tesserae above the disused central heating channels, and the amphorae that had been used to store such luxuries as wine, olives and fish-sauce lay smashed in heaps. The road system was useful, though it sank gradually into disrepair and the villages retreated from the marching-lines of the war-bands. As for laws and law-courts, taxes and tax-collectors – they vanished as completely as the discipline of the legions, so that by the sixth century the author Gildas could solemnly write a history of Britain in ignorance of the very fact that it had been a Roman province for more than three centuries.

Rome had gone, but the Britons remained, and there has been intense debate about the evolution that took place amid the ruins in the fifth and sixth centuries. The Arthurian legends almost certainly perpetuate the story of a resistance struggle; whoever it was that built the great hall at South Cadbury in the late fifth century, the hill fort, like others of its kind, was certainly reoccupied and held by British, rather than Saxon warriors. But we must not be led into romanticising by the magic of names such as Aurelius Ambrosianus or Camelot; Neil Faulkner has acidly remarked that 'A great cultural chasm separated the Dark Age warlords, with their tin badges and inflated titles, who controlled South Cadbury in the late fifth century, from the Roman gentleman-bureaucrats who had run towns like Verulamium [or Corinium] in the early fourth' (*The Decline and Fall of Roman Britain*, Tempus, 2000).

Despite the ignorance of Gildas, this eighth-century poet recognised the work of giants when he saw it.

> *Splendid is this masonry.*
> *The fates destroyed it,*
> *The strong building crashed,*
> *The work of giants moulders away.*
>
> The Ruin
> *An eighth-century Saxon poem*

An impressive pot from a burial site in Selborne.

The evidence of place-names and linguistic survivals suggests a different kind of continuity, which has been described as 'the desertion of the villages but not the disappearance of the Britons' (R.R. Sellman, *Roman Britain*, Methuen, 1961). And the Laws of Alfred, of the late ninth century, show that in Wessex, the Saxon heartland, Welshmen – that is, the descendants of the Romano-Britons – were a distinct group within society, ranging in status from serfs to considerable landowners.

What happened was a process of mingling, lengthy and painful, but not totally or uniformly catastrophic. And eventually Rome returned – this time under the emblem of the cross which Constantine had adopted at the battle of the Milvian Bridge, and which Augustine carried ashore at the legions' old landing-ground in Thanet, in 596.

BIBLIOGRAPHY

Clayton, Peter, *A Companion to Roman Britain*, Phaidon

Collingwood, R.G. and Myres, J.N.L., *Roman Britain and the English Settlements*, Clarendon, Oxford

Dark, P. and K., *The Landscape of Roman Britain*, Sutton, Stroud

Esmonde Cleary, A.S., *The Ending of Roman Britain*, Batsford

Faulkner, Neil, *The Decline and Fall of Roman Britain*, Tempus

Jones, B. and Mattingly, D., *An Atlas of Roman Britain*, Blackwell, Oxford

Leach, Peter, *Roman Somerset*, The Dovecote Press

Putnam, Bill, *The Romans*, The Dovecote Press

Sharples, N. M., *Maiden Castle*, Batsford